Giant of the Desert

by Judy Nayer
illustrated by Gary Torrisi

Harcourt

Orlando   Boston   Dallas   Chicago   San Diego

Visit *The Learning Site!*

www.harcourtschool.com

The saguaro (sə•wär•o) is a giant cactus. Sometimes I think it looks like a giant person, with arms that shoot up to the sky.

The saguaro grows in the Sonoran Desert.

California

Colorado River

Arizona

New Mexico

Sonoran Desert

Mexico

Stems

Roots

How does the saguaro live in the hot and dry desert? It stores lots of water in its stems. Its roots spread out far and wide, too. That way it can soak up the rain that falls.

Spines

The saguaro has sharp spines. The spines keep animals from eating the plant. Even when the plant dies, it does not shed its spines.

If you listen closely, you can hear the tap, tap of a bird making holes in the saguaro. This bird is making a nest.

I hear a little hoot. A tiny owl has moved into an old nest. It hunts at night and sleeps in the nest in the daytime. The nest stays cool even in the hot noon sun.

These birds are called
Harris's hawks.

Big birds make their homes here, too.
These birds roost in a nest of twigs.

The saguaro
blooms in May.

Now it is time for the saguaro to
bloom. Beautiful white and yellow
flowers open up at the tops of
the stems.

When the moon is in the sky, bats come to the saguaro. They drink the sweet juice inside the flowers. This is the bats' food and source of energy.

Doves coo.
Butterflies flit.
Bees zoom.

When the sun comes up, more animals discover the saguaro flowers. They have come for the nectar, too. As they fly from bloom to bloom, they carry pollen with them. The pollen helps the fruit begin to grow.

When the fruit is ripe, people come. They pull the red fruit loose with sticks. They scoop the fruit into buckets. They will cook the fruit to make jam and other foods.

These desert pigs are called javelinas (häv•ə•lē•nəz).

Birds and ants come to eat the saguaro fruit and seeds that have fallen. Coyotes and other animals find food at night.

The storm that was forecast has
arrived. Lightning has knocked the
saguaro to the ground, and it dies.
New animals come to live in the
saguaro. Insects and spiders make
little homes.

Seeds

Seedlings

Two years old

Twelve years old

When one saguaro dies, another one starts its new life. The animals that eat the saguaro fruit take its seeds to new places. A few of them sprout and grow.

A saguaro can live for 200 years or more.

Over many years, the new saguaro grows tall. Flowers bloom and arms start to grow. At last, this plant becomes the giant of the desert.